PRIMARY SOURCES IN AMERICAN HISTORY™

THE OREGON TRAIL

A PRIMARY SOURCE HISTORY OF THE ROUTE TO THE AMERICAN WEST

STEVEN P. OLSON

rosen central
Primary Source™

The Rosen Publishing Group, Inc., New York

To Margaret, who came West, for which I am grateful

Published in 2004 by The Rosen Publishing Group, Inc.
29 East 21st Street, New York, NY 10010

First Edition

Library of Congress Cataloging-in-Publication Data

Olson, Steven P.
The Oregon Trail: a primary source history of the route to the American West/by Steven P. Olson—1st ed.
    p. cm.—(Primary sources in American history)
Summary: Uses primary source documents, narrative, and illustrations to recount the history of the Oregon Trail, its role in westward expansion, and the travails of the pioneers who followed it across the West.
Includes bibliographical references and index.
ISBN 0-8239-4512-X (library binding)
1. Oregon National Historic Trail—Juvenile literature. 2. Overland journeys to the Pacific—Juvenile literature. 3. Frontier and pioneer life—West (U.S.)—Juvenile literature. 4. Frontier and pioneer life—Oregon—Juvenile literature. 5. West (U.S.)—History—19th century—Juvenile literature. 6. Oregon—History—To 1859—Juvenile literature. 7. United States—Territorial expansion—Juvenile literature. [1. Oregon National Historic Trail. 2. Overland journeys to the Pacific. 3. Frontier and pioneer life—West (U.S.) 4. West (U.S.)—History—19th century. 5. United States—Territorial expansion.]
I. Title. II. Series.
F597.O47 2004
979.5'03–dc22

                                             2003011783

Manufactured in the United States of America

On the front cover: *Barlow Cutoff*, a 1930 watercolor painting by William Henry Jackson. From the Scotts Bluff National Monument.

On the back cover: First row (left to right): committee drafting the Declaration of Independence for action by the Continental Congress; Edward Braddock and troops ambushed by Indians at Fort Duquesne. Second row (left to right): the *Mayflower* in Plymouth Harbor; the Oregon Trail at Barlow Cutoff. Third row (left to right): slaves waiting at a slave market; the USS *Chesapeake* under fire from the HMS *Shannon*.

CONTENTS

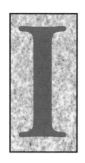

INTRODUCTION

Since the first settlers landed in the New World, Americans have always looked toward the setting sun with hope for a better future. The first Europeans in America quickly moved farther west into river valleys with better farming lands. Their grandchildren crossed the Allegheny Mountains. Their great-great-grandchildren, who were inspired men like Thomas Jefferson, Meriwether Lewis, and Jedediah Smith, blazed the Oregon Trail. And the great-great-grandchildren of those Oregon trailblazers lived in peace along the West Coast of the United States.

OREGON TERRITORY

The busiest path that these trailblazers followed to the West was the Oregon Trail. From towns like St. Louis and Independence in present-day Missouri, settlers left the banks of the mighty Mississippi River and headed west toward the Oregon Territory, which extended from the border of California, east to the Rockies, and far into present-day Canada. Up the Missouri River to the junction with the Platte River, emigrants (people who leave one country or region to settle in another) then marched in a western direction until they crossed the Continental Divide along the South Pass route. At Fort Bridger, some, like Brigham Young and his band of Mormon pioneers, turned south for Utah. California settlers stepped off the Oregon Trail later, at Fort Hall. Those who chose to continue toward

Oregon Territory curled northward along the Snake River into Idaho, through Fort Boise, and over the Bitterroot Range. On the far side of those difficult mountains, settlers picked up the trail along the Clearwater River, which fed into the Columbia River, finally emptying into the Pacific Ocean.

A map cannot illustrate the difficulties of discovering and following the Oregon Trail. When the United States was founded in 1776, white explorers had been up part of the Mississippi River. Some had circled the tip of South America and explored the Pacific Ocean along the West Coast. The territory between these bodies of water was an enormous mystery. Over the next seven decades, the mystery would be solved, bit by bit. No single expedition discovered the best way to come west over land, but each one added something to the body of knowledge, outposts, and landmarks that became known as the Oregon Trail.

Even after the Oregon Trail was marked and known, it was by no means easy to follow. It is estimated that the Oregon Trail claimed 34,000 lives. Some fell from cholera, measles, or other ailments. Some suffered fatal wounds from grizzly bears, mountain lions, or falls over cliffs. Some drowned crossing rivers, while others drowned in pools of quicksand. Rattlesnakes, scorpions, and mosquitoes carrying disease nipped at the ankles of many unfortunates. Beneath the violent thunderstorms of the Midwest, the scathing sandstorms of the Great Plains, and the relentless snowstorms in the Rocky Mountains, some simply wore out. Still others starved to death. Something as simple as a broken wagon wheel could doom a family. The road west was littered with broken wheels, dead animals, wagons half-buried in mud, and many roadside graves.

The Northwest Passage

The first white Americans to look west did not see the land between the Mississippi River and the Pacific Ocean as an opportunity. They saw it as a barrier to be crossed. These explorers hoped to find a river system that connected the Mississippi River to the Pacific Ocean. Such a passage would allow a direct trade route between the East Coast and China, where American pelts could be exchanged for silks, spices, and other goods. This mythical route was called the Northwest Passage.

The Northwest Passage was thought to be connected to the mighty Missouri River, which fed into the Mississippi River. Some, like President Thomas Jefferson, guessed that a short walk over land connected the Missouri River to a river that eventually

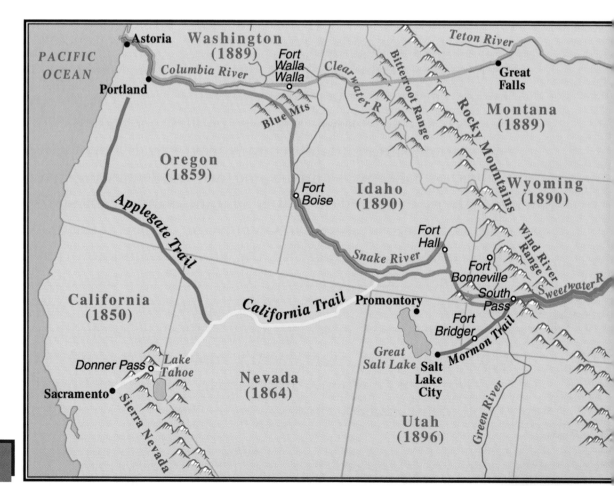

led to the Columbia River in the Oregon Territory. By 1800, Great Britain and the United States had sent explorers into the region in search of this passage. While no one would ever find the Northwest Passage, the race had begun between Great Britain and its former colonies, the United States, to control the very real Oregon Territory.

The Louisiana Purchase

Between the Oregon Territory and the Mississippi River lay an enormous region in which the Northwest Passage was believed to be located. Claimed in 1682 by the French explorer La Salle, the territory of Louisiana was named after King Louis XIV and included the region from the Rocky Mountains in the

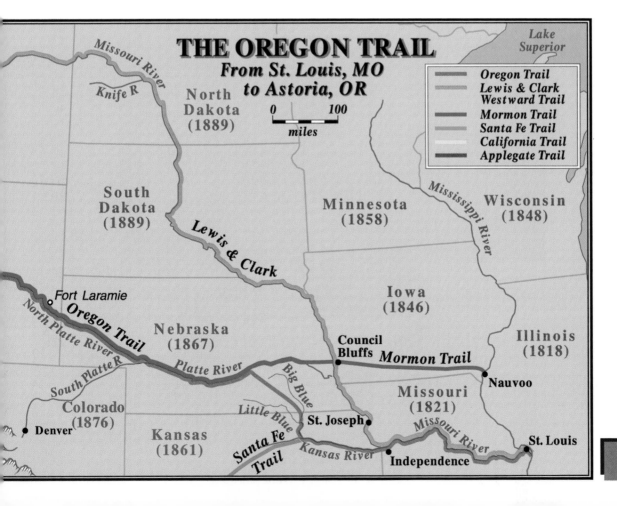

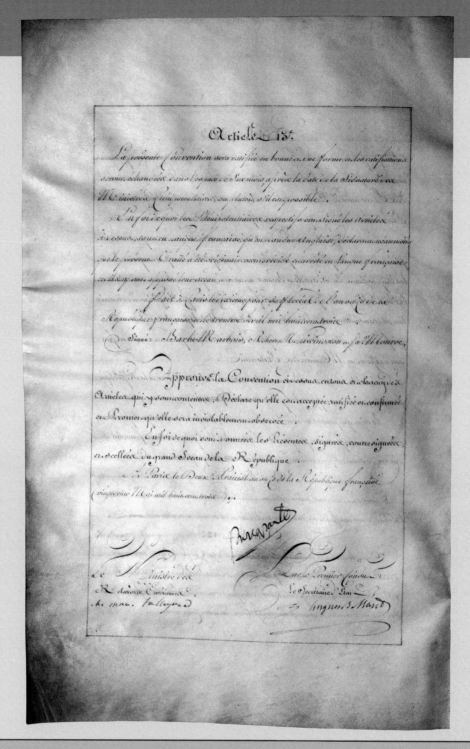

Purchasing the Louisiana Territory from France allowed the United States to expand into a vast area of rich resources. The young country gained 828,000 square miles (2,144,510 square kilometers) of land west of the Mississippi River at the price of approximately three cents per acre—one of the best real estate deals in history. The Louisiana Purchase Treaty *(above)* is made up of three documents: a treaty of cession and two financial conventions. See transcription on page 56.

west and the Appalachian Mountains in the east, north to Canada, and south to the Gulf of Mexico. To the north, Great Britain had secured Canada. To the south, Spain ruled Mexico and had pushed northward into California on the far side of the Rockies. France needed to defend the vast area of Louisiana from the British and Spanish, but that proved difficult because it was so far away.

In controlling the Louisiana Territory, France became a neighbor to the United States. In 1800, President Thomas Jefferson was very nervous to have France next door. Jefferson's armies could neither take Louisiana by force nor resist a French invasion. Through his minister in Paris, Jefferson began discussions to purchase New Orleans, the port city at the mouth of the Mississippi River. France was not interested in selling.

By January 1802, Emperor Napoléon had decided to protect French lands in North America and assembled two armies to do so. The first army was wiped out by yellow fever on the island of San Domingo in the Caribbean Sea. When the second army arrived to reinforce the first, it also fell to yellow fever and attacks from hostile natives. Since it was nearly impossible to defend both France and Louisiana without those armies, Emperor Napoléon agreed to sell Louisiana to the United States.

On December 20, 1803, the U.S. flag was raised in New Orleans. For a total of $15,000,000, President Jefferson had purchased a vast territory that white men had barely explored. When an American negotiator asked French minister Charles-Maurice de Talleyrand how far Louisiana extended, Talleyrand replied, "I do not know." Jefferson intended to find out.

TIMELINE

1803

On December 20, President Thomas Jefferson purchases the Louisiana Territory from France, doubling the size of the United States, for three cents an acre.

1804

President Jefferson hires Captain Meriwether Lewis to explore the Louisiana Territory and map a route to the Pacific Ocean. On May 14, Lewis's Corps of Discovery leaves St. Louis, sailing up the Missouri River.

1805

On November 7, the Corps of Discovery reaches the mouth of the Columbia River in present-day Oregon. They are the first Americans to reach the Pacific over land.

1806

On September 23, the Corps of Discovery returns to St. Louis as heroes.

1812

On October 22, Robert Stuart leads his party eastward from Astoria, Oregon, through the South Pass in the Wind River Range, marking a critical portion of the Oregon Trail that thousands of wagons and horses would later follow.

TIMELINE

1832 — Captain Benjamin Bonneville leads the first caravan across the Continental Divide over the South Pass in the Wind River Range in Wyoming.

1843 — The Great Migration of 1843 becomes the first caravan to bring settlers across the entire 2,000 miles (3,219 km) of the Oregon Trail.

1845 — New York newspaper man John L. O'Sullivan coins the term "manifest destiny," which proclaims the belief that North America should be governed as one nation, the United States.

1846 — On June 15, the Oregon Treaty fixes the border between the United States and British territory at the forty-ninth parallel. Most of the Oregon Territory becomes American.

1846 — In the winter of 1846–1847, the Donner-Reed wagon train becomes snowbound crossing the Sierra Nevada. When they are rescued in February 1847, only half of the original party is still alive.

TIMELINE

January 24, 1847 — James Marshall discovers a nugget of gold at Sutter's Mill in the foothills of California. The California gold rush begins.

July 24, 1847 — Brigham Young leads the first group of Mormons into the Great Salt Lake area.

February 2, 1848 — The war between the United States and Mexico ends. California and other territories of the Southwest are sold to the United States for $15,000,000.

1850 — Congress passes the Oregon Donation Land Law, which allows a family to claim up to 640 acres (259 hectares) of Oregon land.

September 9, 1850 — California becomes the thirty-first state of the Union.

February 14, 1859 — Oregon is admitted as the thirty-third state of the Union.

May 10, 1869 — A gold spike is driven into the transcontinental railroad at Promontory, Utah, connecting the East to the West via rail. Overland trails like the Oregon Trail begin to disappear.

CHAPTER 1

On January 18, 1803, Thomas Jefferson asked Congress for $2,500 to cover the costs of an expedition "to explore the Missouri River, & such principal streams of it, as, by its course & communication with the waters of the Pacific Ocean, may offer the most direct & practicable communication across this continent, for the purposes of commerce."

LEWIS AND CLARK AND THE CORPS OF DISCOVERY

Jefferson longed to send an American expedition through the Louisiana Territory to find the Northwest Passage to the Pacific Ocean and to China beyond it. And he had found the man to lead it.

Army captain Meriwether Lewis had grown up on the farm next to Thomas Jefferson's estate in Virginia. A skilled man of the frontier, Lewis had also received training from leading American scientists in botany and zoology. Fortunately, Lewis was wise enough to select an able lieutenant to help him reach the Pacific.

William Clark could not have been more different from Meriwether Lewis. Where Lewis was a loner who became angered easily, the calmer Clark liked to talk among the men. Lewis had scientific training, and Clark was a fine navigator,

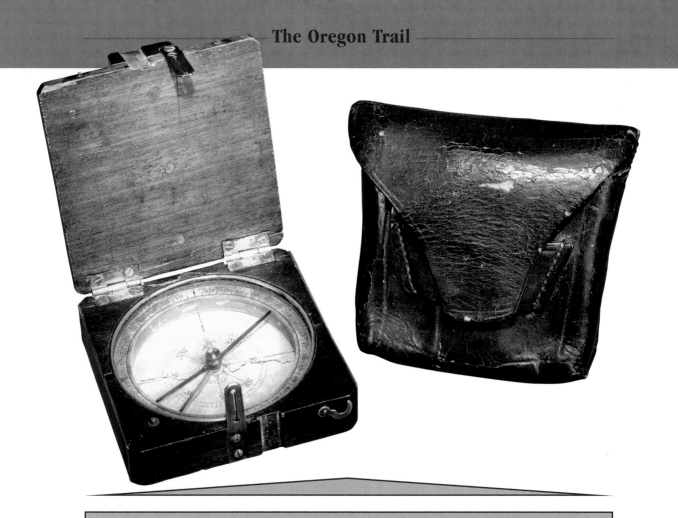

Meriwether Lewis purchased the compass and leather case shown above from Thomas Whitney's Philadelphia shop for $23.50, according to Lewis's journal. Used by William Clark to navigate the route on Lewis and Clark's famous expedition, the compass is made from silver and brass and has a paper dial. It is set in a mahogany box, which fits inside the leather case. During the expedition, Clark lost the compass in a flash flood but recovered it the next day. He later gave it to U.S. Army captain Robert A. McCabe, who passed it down through his family. The compass can now be found in the National Museum of American History, in Washington, D.C.

mapmaker, and boatman. Both were good judges of character. Each man they selected for the expedition was an able frontiersman with a useful skill such as carpentry, blacksmithing, or hunting. In time, Lewis and Clark shaped their men into a well-organized unit. Together, they would become the greatest explorers in American history: the Corps of Discovery.

The Adventure Begins

On May 14, 1804, the Corps of Discovery left the town of St. Louis. They traveled up the mouth of the Missouri River in two canoes and a sail-powered keelboat. In the first days, little was heard but the songs of birds and the splashing of oars. Deer and elk roamed the riverbank and showed no fear of the men in boats. The men hunted and fished and ate their catch with a daily allowance of cornmeal and four ounces (1.2 deciliters) of whiskey.

Yet travel was not without hazards. On this part of the journey, ticks and mosquitoes nipped at the explorers every day. The boats had troubles, too, as they were grounded on sandbars, rammed by logs, or snagged by overhanging tree branches. Near the mouth of the Teton River, three teenagers of the Lakota Nation paddled out to meet the boat. Their chiefs wanted to meet with the chief of the corps. Lewis gave the chiefs whiskey and tobacco, but it was not enough. After a tense argument, the corps left, narrowly escaping a terrible fight.

On October 24, the Corps of Discovery stepped off the boats at a Mandan village at the juncture of the Missouri and the Knife Rivers in present-day North Dakota. They found a pair of peaceful tribes living in sturdy earthen lodges and working in healthy gardens.

In response to the good cheer and help provided by the Corps of Discovery, the Mandan invited them to build a fort across the river for the winter. A blacksmith had brought his forge on the trip, and he was able to exchange repair of the tribe's knives and kettles for much-needed corn and buffalo meat. During the bitterly cold winter, there were regular visits between the Mandan and the Americans.

Living among the Mandan was a French trader, Toussaint Charbonneau, and his teenaged bride, Sacagawea. A member of

Recapitulation of an estimate of the sum
necessary to carry into effect the Miss[a]
expedition. —

Mathematical Instruments	$. 217.
Arms & Accoutrements extraordinary	". 81.
Camp Equipage	". 255.
Medecine & packing	". 55.
Means of transportation	". 430.
Indian presents	". 696.
Provisions extraordinary	". 224.
Materials for making up the various articles into portable packs	". 55.
For the pay of hunters guides & Interpreters	". 300.
In silver coin to defray the expences of the party from Nashville to the last white settlement on the Missourie	". 100.
Contingencies	". 87.
Total	$.2,500.

19946

Meriwether Lewis drew up this estimate of expedition costs and submitted it to Thomas Jefferson on April 20, 1803. The total amount requested by Lewis was $2,500. The largest amount requested—even greater than the money requested for transportation—was allotted for "Indian presents," which were critical to gaining the assistance of various Native American guides whom Lewis and Clark needed for their journey.

the Shoshone tribe who had been sold to Charbonneau, Sacagawea gave birth to their first child, a boy, on February 11, 1805. Captain Lewis assisted in the delivery. The new parents wanted to leave the Mandan camp in the spring with the expedition. Lewis agreed, as he was sure that Sacagawea could assist them as a translator. Sacagawea spoke both Shoshone and Hidatsa.

As Clark noted in his diary on October 19, 1805: "The wife of Shabono [Charbonneau] our interpreter we find reconciles all the Indians, as to our friendly intentions a woman with a party of men is a token of peace." When the expedition entered Shoshone lands, Sacagawea recognized landmarks from her childhood and discovered the correct branches of the Missouri River to follow. At other times, she was able to find edible roots, such as white artichoke, to add to the group's diet. When scientific instruments and journals fell from her husband's canoe, she calmly retrieved them.

She accomplished all of this while nursing and carrying a baby boy. For her abilities and strength, she earned the respect of the men of the corps. While we know very little about what she looked like or her fate after the expedition, we do know that she was a vital part of the journey.

To the Pacific

On April 7, 1805, the Corps of Discovery left its winter camp in canoes and headed into the unknown. As Lewis noted in his journal:

> We were now about to penetrate a country ... on which the foot of civilized man had never trodden; the good or evil it had in store for us was for experiment yet to determine, and these little vessells contained every article by which we were expected to subsist or defend ourselves.

Sacagawea is portrayed here in a drawing by E. S. Paxson in a pose of strength and unity with nature. The daughter of a Shoshone chief, Sacagawea was kidnapped from her tribe by the Mandan. She was purchased by the French Canadian trapper Toussaint Charbonneau, who wed her and fathered her son, Jean Baptiste. Sacagawea was an invaluable addition to the Corps of Discovery. The details of Sacagawea's later life are uncertain, but it is known that Jean Baptiste was sent to live with William Clark, who raised and educated him.

Into Montana, the corps pushed upriver, fighting terrible sandstorms that raked their faces like sandpaper. Lewis had been warned by the Mandan of an animal twice as tall as a man. On April 29, Lewis was chased by such an animal. It was a grizzly bear, "a much more furious and formidable animal," which another corpsmen shot several times before it died. Within a week, Lewis wrote that "the curiossity of our party is pretty well satisfied with rispect to this anamal."

Despite the trials of the trail, Lewis and Clark saw many natural wonders along the Missouri. They found 200-foot (61-meter) cliffs of such a thin and regular shape that Lewis noted in his diary that "nature had attempted here to rival the human art of masonry." The men noted pronghorn antelope, prairie dogs, coyotes, and other species that had never been documented by white men. The herds of buffalo were so thick that the prairies appeared to be black.

While Clark liked to remain with the men paddling up the Missouri, Lewis walked along the banks of the river ahead of them, often alone, and collected plant and animal samples. As predicted by the Mandan, Lewis arrived at the first great barrier to their passage, which he described in his diary: "[M]y ears were saluted with the agreeable sound of a fall of water and advancing a little further I saw the spray arrise above the plain like a collumn of smoke . . . a roaring too tremendious to be mistaken for any cause short of the great falls of the Missouri."

The Mandan had said that carrying canoes and their keelboat up the Great Falls would take half a day. Two days later, the men were repairing their shoes and looking up at more waterfalls to climb. It took twenty-four days to reach calm water above the falls.

The lengthy climb had been a dangerous delay. To be stuck in the Rocky Mountains to the west during winter could be fatal. As Lewis noted in his journal: "[W]e begin to feel considerable anxiety with rispect to the Snake [Shoshone] Indians. If we do not find them or some other nation who have horses I fear the successfull issue of our voyage will be very doubtfull."

Lewis led his men to the headwaters of the mighty Missouri River, which had shrunk to a small creek that could be straddled by a man. Abandoning their boats, the expedition then began climbing into the mountains on foot. When they reached the top of a ridge, they discovered on the far side more and more mountains in all directions. At that moment,

Captains Lewis & Clark holding a Council with the Indians

Among the greatest accomplishments of the Lewis and Clark expedition were the relationships they forged with Native Americans. Lewis and Clark held many councils with Native American groups, which was the start of formal relations between the United States and Western tribes. Thomas Jefferson coached the two men on approaching and relating with the Native Americans whom they would meet on their travels. Their mission was to explain that, according to the Louisiana Purchase, the United States owned the land occupied by the Native Americans. They were also to arrange trade agreements and form military alliances with Native American tribes.

the dream of a Northwest Passage died. With so many mountains in front of them, the search for the Shoshone and their horses became desperate.

On August 13, 1805, Meriwether Lewis spied three Shoshone women with their children. Lewis put his gun down and slowly approached them, gave them beads and mirrors, and painted vermillion on their faces as a sign of peace. They took him to their village. When the remainder of the expedition arrived, one of the corps members reported that Sacagawea "instantly jummped up, and ran and embraced [the chief], throwing over him her blanket and weeping profusely." The chief was her brother.

Over the course of an entire day, Lewis and the chief negotiated for the horses. The chief spoke to Sacagawea in Shoshone, who spoke to Charbonneau in Hidatsa, the language of the Mandan. Charbonneau spoke to one of the men in French, who spoke to Lewis in English. Then, Lewis's reply had to be passed back. Eventually, the Corps of Discovery had their horses.

Without those horses, their crossing of the Bitterroot Range in present-day Idaho would have been fatal. These "most terrible mountains," as Lewis described them in his diary, were already covered in deep snow. Their Shoshone guide got lost. The party ran out of food, and they were forced to eat candle wax and, eventually, their horses. Eleven days later and on the verge of death, the party stumbled to the banks of the Clearwater River in present-day Idaho. The water in it flowed to the west. They had crossed the Continental Divide. No white American had crossed the divide on foot.

Camping near them was a tribe of Nez Percé. The Nez Percé taught the white men how to build dugout canoes, and off they paddled, abandoning their horses. Down the Clearwater, they reached the Snake River in eastern Washington. On October 16, they reached the Columbia River. The men woke one morning to see the Pacific Ocean behind the lifting fog.

Returning Heroes

President Jefferson had given Lewis a letter guaranteeing payment to any ship captain who returned the expedition to the United States. When no ship arrived to take them back, Lewis

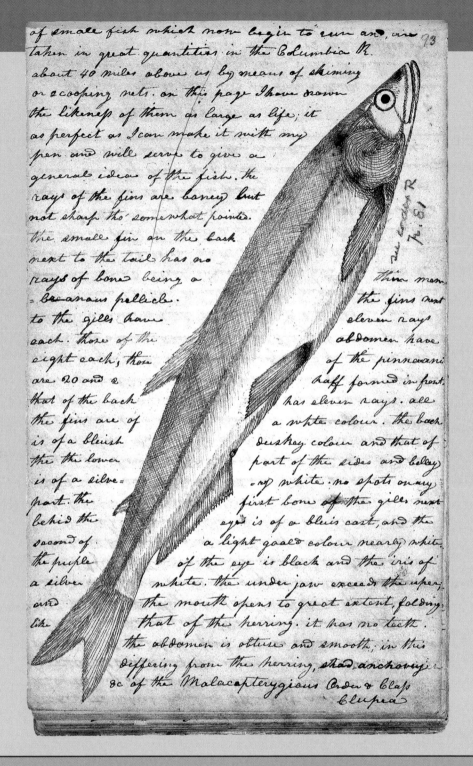

Lewis and Clark kept extensive journals on their journey, which provided valuable information about the people, land, and wildlife of the West. The page shown here describes the eulachon (*Thaleichthys pacificus*) and includes a sketch of the fish. The entries are highly detailed: "The first bone of the gills next behind the eyes is of a bluis[h] cast, and the second of a light [gold] colour nearly white. The [pupil] of the eye is black and the iris of a silver white."

and Clark decided that everyone in the group, including Sacagawea, a woman, and York, a black slave, should have a vote in deciding where to camp for the winter. Such a vote would not be legal in America for another 114 years.

The Corps of Discovery headed back up the Columbia on March 23, 1806. Because they knew the route and what to expect, the men had a much easier time getting back. Their Shoshone guide led them through a shortcut that saved forty-nine days. In September, they reached the Mandan villages and left Sacagawea and her family there.

On September 23, 1806, the Corps of Discovery drifted down the Missouri River and into the town of St. Louis where, according to Lewis's diary entry for that day, they "were met by all the village and received a harty welcom from it's inhabitants." These heroes had traveled more than 8,000 miles (12,875 km), encountered more than 50 Native American tribes, and recorded 110 new animal species and 170 plant species. They had final proof that the Northwest Passage did not exist. They had suffered only one death, a young soldier who died of fever. Although the path of their expedition took them farther north of what eventually became the Oregon Trail, Lewis and Clark had proven that an overland crossing to the Pacific was possible.

Lewis returned to Washington, D.C., to present his findings to President Jefferson. One can only imagine their meeting in the Oval Office, as these two great men spread the most valuable treasure of the expedition on the floor between them. With that map, they dreamed of building a nation that stretched to the Pacific. Those dreams would become a united country connected by the Oregon Trail.

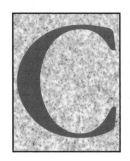

CHAPTER 2

Before he could publish the journals of his expedition, Meriwether Lewis died in 1809. However, information about the journey was already spreading by word of mouth. Such tales reached the ears of John Jacob Astor, a German fur trader who believed that another fortune in fur could be made in the Pacific Northwest.

Robert Stuart

In 1810, Astor funded an expedition to explore the Oregon Territory. His ship, the *Tonquin*, sailed around the tip of South America and up the West Coast of America. At the mouth of the Columbia River in present-day Oregon, Astor's men founded a town called Astoria. While under attack by a group of Native Americans in Canadian waters, the ship was blown up by accident, and all aboard were killed.

By June 1812, no resupply ship had come to Astoria, and the remaining men decided that a group of them must travel over land to report to Astor and acquire new supplies. As their leader, they selected Robert Stuart, a sturdy and fair Scotsman. Stuart's journal began: "In the afternoon of Monday the 29th June 1812, we sailed from Astoria, under a salute of cannon from the Fort." On the lower part of the Columbia River, Stuart noted large trees, good farming land, and many beavers.

MARKING THE TRAIL

Born the son of a German butcher, John Jacob Astor (1763–1848) immigrated to the United States in 1783. Soon, he was established in the fur industry. His company, American Fur Company, was the first business monopoly in the United States. His desire to expand his fortune in the West drove him to fund an expedition to explore the Oregon Territory. Astor's wealth was bolstered by his investments in New York City real estate, and real estate continued the Astor family legacy for years to come.

When the Columbia turned north, Stuart and his party followed a southeasterly route by horse across dry hill country into present-day Idaho. By September, the chilly air had turned quite cold. According to Stuart's diary, he awoke one morning to the sound of stampeding hooves.

One of the [Crow Indian] party rode past our camp and placed himself on a conspicuous knob, in the direction they wanted to run [the horses] off; when the others (who were hidden behind our camp), seeing him prepared, rose the war-whoop ... the animals naturally rose their heads to see what the matter was—at that instant he who had planted himself in advance put spurs to his steed, and ours, seeing him gallop off in apparent fright, started all in the same direction, as if a legion of infernals were in pursuit of them ...

Crow braves had stolen all of their horses. Staring winter in the face, the men had no choice but to pick up the loads of their horses and set out on foot.

By late October, Stuart and his group had reached western Wyoming, where a long ridge of mountains blocked their path. Stuart searched until he found a pass low enough to walk over. On the far side, Stuart noted in his diary, "the country in every direction South of east is a plain, bounded only by the horizon." This route through the Wind River Range, known then and now as South Pass, would become the gateway to the Northwest.

Eventually, Stuart found his way to the Sweetwater River, which fed into the Platte River in present-day Wyoming. On April 30, 1813, Stuart arrived in St. Louis: "We a little before sun set reached the Town of St. Louis, all in the most perfect health, after a voyage of ten months from Astoria." Although he did not know it at the time, Stuart had marked a critical leg of what would become the Oregon Trail.

The Forgotten Route

Although a wagon route had been charted through South Pass and on to the Oregon Territory, few dared to cross the vast prairie lands known at the time as the Great American Desert. In 1806, Lieutenant Zebulon M. Pike had explored the central region of the Louisiana Territory and advised his superiors to leave it to the Native Americans. In 1819, Major Stephen H. Long and his exploring party reached the same conclusion. While food was plentiful in the form of buffalo, the flat and featureless grasslands offered little water or shade. The overland trail west was forgotten by most.

Lieutenant Zebulon Montgomery Pike (1779–1813) published his accounts of his expeditions to the West under the title *An Account of Expeditions to the Sources of the Mississippi*. Pike wrote that there were "tracts of many leagues where the wind had thrown up the sand in all the fanciful form of the ocean's rolling wave; and on which not a speck of vegetable matter existed." Such descriptions inhibited Western migration for half a century.

Jedediah Smith

In February 1822, General William H. Ashley placed an ad in a Missouri newspaper looking for 100 men "to ascend the river Missouri to its source, there to be employed one, two, or three years." Responding to the ad was Jedediah Smith, a tall mountain man with experience trapping and exploring in the West. Less than a year later, he was the leader of the 100 men.

In the following year, General Ashley ordered Smith and ten men to trap animals for their pelts in the interior of the Rocky Mountains. Leaving Fort Kiowa in South Dakota, Smith and his men headed west up the White River and through the Black Hills. Despite being mauled by a grizzly bear, Smith managed to lead the group to a Crow winter camp in the foothills of the Wind River Range. While trading with the friendly Crows, Smith wanted to know where they found their excellent beaver pelts. In piles of sand representing the mountains, the chief of the Crows indicated a low area between two mountains. In February, Smith and

This Frederic Remington painting shows Jedediah Smith leading a line of men on horseback through the dusty Western landscape. Born in New York State in 1798, Smith made numerous trips west as a young man. Like other mountain men, he learned the lay of the land, befriended Indians, and became heavily influenced by them. As well as serving on expeditions, many mountain men acted as guides to the settlers who gradually came west. As the area became increasingly civilized, the mountain men's way of life disappeared. Smith was killed by the Comanche in 1831.

his men struggled through deep snow along the Sweetwater River to a wide slope that was free of snow. Up the slope and down the far side, Smith broke through the ice in a creek to discover that its water flowed to the west. While Robert Stuart had traveled it from west to east, Jedediah Smith had marked the South Pass route from the eastern direction. Its location was spread to trappers and other mountain men, who would later lead caravans through it and across the Continental Divide. This time, the South Pass was not forgotten.

A strong leader, Smith pioneered many methods of travel in caravans. At dawn, scouts rode ahead to plan the day's travels. When they came back, the rest of the camp headed out, with small

Artists made their way west and sent back drawings and paintings of the landscape to represent the area to the eastern part of the country. William Henry Jackson (1843–1942) was one such artist. The above painting, *The Oregon Trail Beyond Devil's Gate*, was inspired by his journey along the Oregon Trail while he was employed by a freighting outfit looking for gold. Later, Jackson captured scenes of the construction of the Union Pacific Railroad and became the foremost photographer of Yellowstone National Park.

scouting parties to all sides of the caravan. Using these methods, larger caravans were rarely attacked. In 1826, the members of his group became the first white men to cross from California back over the Sierra Nevada. Smith continued to explore the West until 1831 when he was killed by a group of Comanche in New Mexico.

Native Americans

In his instructions for the journey to the Pacific, President Thomas Jefferson cautioned Meriwether Lewis to treat the Native Americans "in the most friendly & conciliatory manner which their own conduct will admit." Lewis wisely followed those words.

On June 20, 1803, Thomas Jefferson wrote this letter of detailed instructions to Meriwether Lewis before his important expedition. "The object of your mission," Jefferson wrote, "is to explore the Missouri river, & such principal stream of it as by it's course and communication with the waters of the Pacific ocean whether the Columbia, Oregon, Colorado or any other river may offer the most direct & practicable water communication across this continent for the purposes of commerce." He also instructed Lewis on how to treat the Native Americans he would meet. These instructions served Lewis well but were rarely followed by subsequent expeditions. See partial transcription on pages 56–57.

While the first caravans on the Oregon Trail had good relations with the Native Americans, later caravans slaughtered herds of buffalo on which the Native Americans depended. White farmers claimed and fenced off lands through which the Native Americans had long migrated. In turn, native groups sought tariffs from white caravans to pass through their lands or stole horses, guns, blankets, and food from sleeping settlers. And white people brought diseases to the native tribes. When measles wiped out half of a Cayuse tribe, its braves blamed Dr. Marcus Whitman and massacred him and his family. The army, in turn, waged war on the Cayuse. Eventually, all Native American tribes were killed off or herded onto reservations.

The Oregon Question

In 1832, Captain Benjamin Bonneville led the first wagon train over the South Pass into a grassy meadow along the Green River in present-day Wyoming. He and his 110 men built a simple fort and scattered into beaver country to collect pelts and trade with Native Americans.

Bonneville took careful notes on the region, his travels, and the men who passed his fort. Many of them were British. Bonneville's notes were passed to the U.S. government.

Although the United States and Britain had agreed to share the Oregon Territory, people in government still debated whether the United States should fight Britain over "the Oregon question." In 1837, Washington Irving wrote *The Adventures of Captain Bonneville*, which opened the Oregon question to the American public.

CHAPTER 3

TRAILBLAZERS

In 1837, the economy fell into a depression. Farmers were forced to charge low prices for their products. As a result, many lost their farms because they could not afford to pay their bank loans. Without farmers to buy their goods, small businesses went bankrupt. Seeing farms and businesses closing their doors, many Americans panicked and ran to their banks to get their money. Their banks had already closed their doors for good. The panic of 1837 ruined many families.

The bad times in the East made the Oregon Trail even more appealing. Artists such as Alfred Jacob Miller accompanied expeditions to the West and returned with beautiful portraits and landscapes. Explorers returning from travels to the West spread word of their adventures. In 1838, Oregon missionary Jason Lee came east to plead for more settlers and government support in the Oregon Territory. Lee gave speeches and revived interest in

Once word spread that the American West was a land of great opportunity, individuals and families packed their belongings into wagons and hit the Oregon Trail. Although they were seeking better lives, the journey itself proved difficult and often deadly. After the trauma of leaving family and friends behind, perhaps forever, travelers had to contend with an uncomfortable ride, floods, excessive dust, disease, and the threat of attacks by Native Americans. This photograph shows a National Park Service reenactment of wagons traveling on the Oregon Trail near Scotts Bluff, Nebraska.

the West. Eastern "Oregon Societies" began to form to plan for the day when their caravan would hit the trail.

Hard times continued into the 1840s. As he noted in his trip diary, Missouri farmer Jesse Applegate looked west because the depression "created much discontent and restlessness among a people who had for many generations been nomadic, and had been taught by the example of their ancestors to seek a home in a 'new country' as a sure way of bettering their condition."

Jesse Applegate and the Great Migration of 1843

By the spring of 1843, the Missouri towns of Independence and St. Joseph were bustling with people eager to head west. From these dusty and crowded towns, settlers would begin the overland crossing on the Oregon Trail. Tons of supplies were offloaded from steamboats and quickly sold to settlers who were outfitting their "prairie schooner" wagons. The first large caravan of settlers, the Great Migration of 1843, began to build.

At the trail head in Independence, Missouri, an emigrant family could abandon its heavy Conestoga wagon for a much lighter prairie schooner. These narrow wagons were about fifteen feet (4.6 m) long. Built from sturdy hardwood, the wagon body rode on wooden wheels with tires made of iron. Cotton fabric was double-layered over bent iron hoops to cover the wagon, and the outside layer was oiled and stretched below the rim of the wagon's wood to block rain and sand.

Much lighter than the Conestoga, prairie schooners could be drawn by teams of four oxen, which were stronger than the usual six-horse teams. These red, white, and blue wagons carried thousands of families, their possessions, and their hopes into the West.

Most emigrants spent about $700 to outfit their wagons for the five-month trip. Sacks of flour, bacon, sugar, coffee, beans, rice, salt, and pepper were the basic food supplies. Cooking equipment usually included a small oven, an iron skillet, pots for tea or coffee, and various plates, cups, forks, knives, and spoons. To repair the wagon, tools and replacement parts had to be packed. Each person was allowed a few sets of clothing, and a single tent might cover the entire family at night. For hunting and protection, each wagon took a rifle, pistols, and ammunition. Items such as candles, soap, medicines, and sewing kits were worth far more than their weight. Some families tried to pack furniture and family treasures, but more often than not, these items ended up on the side of the trail.

When a wagon was loaded, it moved to the tent camps on the outskirts of town. One morning, the leader of the caravan would stand on the seat of his wagon and yell, "Turn out! Turn out!" A fleet of red, white, and blue wagons sailed out onto the prairie.

Many of the people heading west were city folk with little frontier experience. Quarrels broke out every day in the wagon train. Families that did not bring cattle refused to guard others' cattle at night. To solve the problem, a caravan of settlers with cattle separated from the main group. Named the Cow Column, this group used the same guides, but was responsible for keeping up with the main column. With several thousand cows in tow, it was a challenge.

The leader of the Cow Column was Jesse Applegate. According to his diary of the journey, a day on the Oregon Trail began at 4:00 AM when rifles were shot into the air. Herders

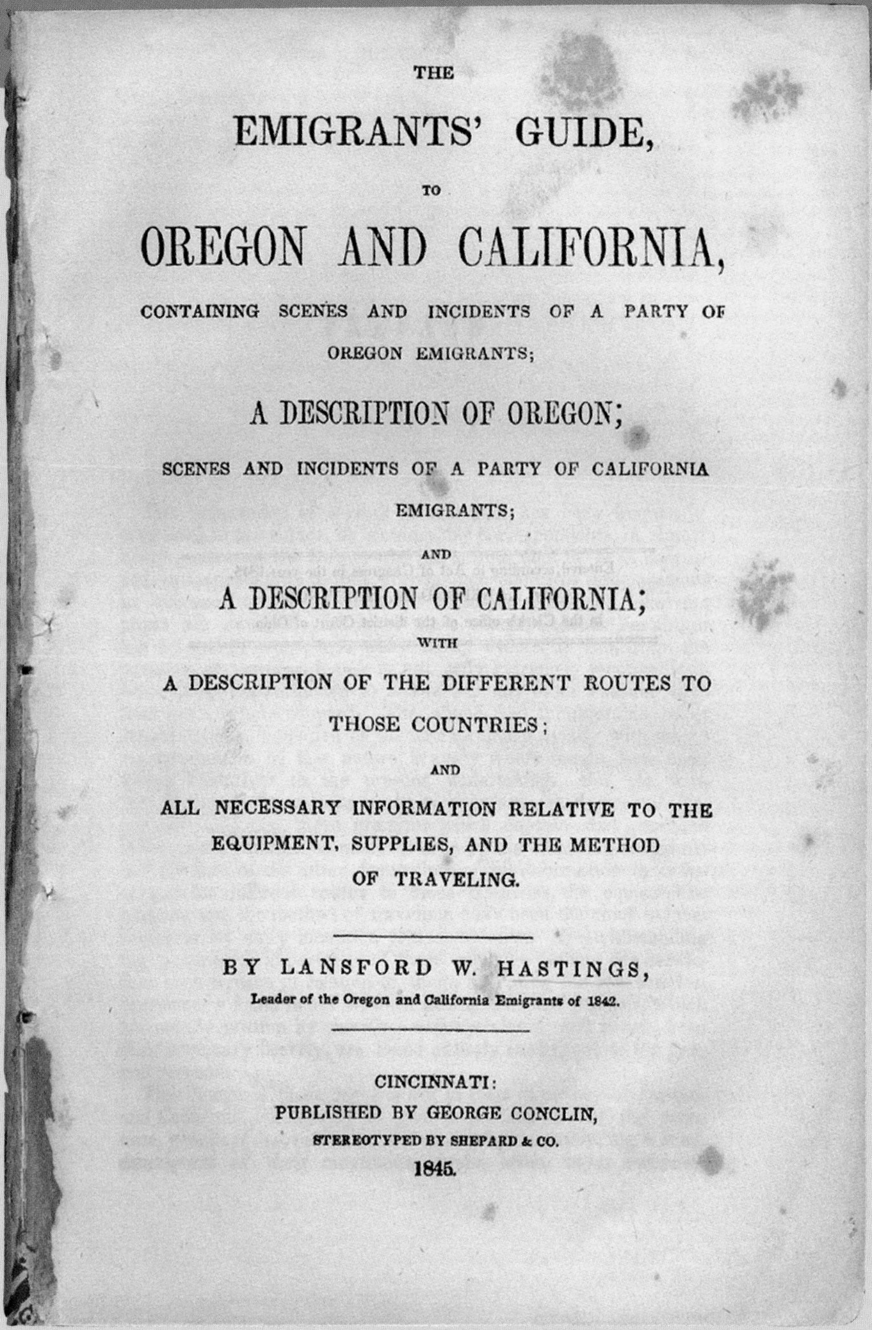

THE

EMIGRANTS' GUIDE,

TO

OREGON AND CALIFORNIA,

CONTAINING SCENES AND INCIDENTS OF A PARTY OF

OREGON EMIGRANTS;

A DESCRIPTION OF OREGON;

SCENES AND INCIDENTS OF A PARTY OF CALIFORNIA

EMIGRANTS;

AND

A DESCRIPTION OF CALIFORNIA;

WITH

A DESCRIPTION OF THE DIFFERENT ROUTES TO

THOSE COUNTRIES;

AND

ALL NECESSARY INFORMATION RELATIVE TO THE
EQUIPMENT, SUPPLIES, AND THE METHOD
OF TRAVELING.

———————

BY LANSFORD W. HASTINGS,

Leader of the Oregon and California Emigrants of 1842.

———————

CINCINNATI:
PUBLISHED BY GEORGE CONCLIN,
STEREOTYPED BY SHEPARD & CO.
1845.

The Emigrants' Guide to Oregon and California, shown above, was written by Lansford W. Hastings in 1845. Hastings traveled to Oregon and California as a young man and decided that the latter state had great potential for development. When he returned east, he wrote the guide to promote westward migration, and he did so in a heavy-handed manner, implying that riches could be found without much effort. Hastings was so focused on convincing people to move west that he neglected to write an accurate guide for emigrating. His recommendation to use a shortcut he called the Hastings Cut-Off was responsible for the tragedy experienced by the Donner party.

gathered the cattle and moved them toward the wagons. Breakfast was made and served. By 7:00 AM, the breakfast dishes were washed and stowed, and the wagons and cattle began to move forward.

The Cow Column stopped for lunch to feed the settlers and water their animals. At noon, settlers might try to collect water and wood for the evening campfire. The train rolled again in the afternoon, stopping at 5:00 PM for the day. Because of the threats of theft by Native Americans or coyotes, wagons were circled in small groups called messes. Oxen and horses were tethered for the night. Around the campfire, families gathered for prayers, listened to sermons, and sang songs. Guards kept an eye and an ear out for threats. At sunup, the day repeated itself.

Caravans that assembled in Independence or St. Joseph crossed over land to the Kansas River and then up the smaller Blue River on a shortcut pioneered by Jedediah Smith. Through a wide valley in Nebraska flowed the gentle Platte River, and buffalo herds fed on the plentiful grass. Here, the Oregon Trail coursed along the North Platte to Fort Laramie in Wyoming. After resting their animals and fixing their wagons, caravans climbed up the Sweetwater River into the foothills of the Rockies and then over the South Pass at 7,500 feet (2,286 m) in elevation.

On the far side of the Continental Divide in the Green River valley, the trail turned northwest and then due north into the hot and dry plains of Idaho. At Fort Hall, those bound for California turned southwest toward the Sierra Nevada. The Oregon Trail continued along the rocky, dusty banks of the Snake River.

The worst parts of the trail came last, when travelers and animals were exhausted. West of Fort Boise in present-day Idaho, the trail crawled over the rocky Snake River plateau, down the Burnt

View of the Chasm through which the Platte issues from the Rocky Mountains.

The North American Continental Divide, shown here in an 1823 engraving, is the highland in the Rocky Mountains that separates the waters that flow toward the Atlantic Ocean from the waters flowing toward the Pacific. Like many others, President Thomas Jefferson believed westward-flowing and eastward-flowing rivers were separated by a short land crossing. Lewis and Clark's inability to find this mythical Northwest Passage forever changed people's understanding about the geography in the West.

River Canyon, and over the Blue Mountains to reach the Columbia River. Applegate managed to lead his caravan to Fort Walla Walla in what is now southern Washington, where he sold the family's cattle and built boats for the trip to the coast. As the Applegates approached a set of rapids on the Columbia, one of the boats drifted too far into the river and was capsized in the rapids. Many years later, Jesse's brother, Lindsay, wrote in a memoir of watching the drowning of two Applegate boys: "At the time of the disaster, it was utterly impossible to render them any assistance for it was only with the greatest skill that we succeeded in saving the women and children from sharing the same fate. It was a painful scene beyond description."

The rest of the family reached the safety of the Willamette Valley in Oregon. So that other families could avoid a similar tragedy on the Columbia, Jesse and Lindsay Applegate pioneered a new trail into southern Oregon in 1846. The Applegate Trail avoided the worst parts at the end of the Oregon Trail.

Manifest Destiny

In 1844, the year after the Great Migration, more caravans headed west, some turning southwest toward California. By 1845, 5,000 people were on the trail. Newspaperman John L. O'Sullivan wrote that it was America's "manifest Destiny" to govern all of North America. The phrase "manifest destiny" became a siren that called Americans into action to conquer the West for the United States. That steady stream of travelers would soon become a flood along the Oregon Trail.

 **C**HAPTER 4

In 1845, the territory west of the Rockies was still divided. The southern part, which included California, was governed by Mexico. The northern part, the Oregon Territory, was divided between the United States and Canada, then a territory of Great Britain. Aware of the rising tide of Americans in Oregon, Great Britain agreed to part with most of the Oregon Territory in 1846. In a treaty approved on June 15 by the U.S. Senate, the border between the United States and Canada was set at the forty-ninth parallel, where it remains to this day.

THE MASS MIGRATION

Many in the area claimed by Mexico wanted to join the United States as well. President James K. Polk sent General Zachary Taylor to form an army in Texas, and the Mexican-American War (1846–1848), also known as the U.S.-Mexican War, was on. Despite fighting in the West, Americans still listened to the call, "Go West, young man!"

The Mormons

In September 1845, the Mormon community of Lima, Illinois, was burned to the ground by rival religious groups. The Mormons' leader, Brigham Young, had had enough. Unpopular with other Christians for their differing beliefs, the Mormons had been chased out of New York, Ohio, and now Illinois. In a letter,

This print by Carl Nebel illustrates the April 18, 1847, Battle of Cerro Gordo during the Mexican-American War. As a result of the war, the United States gained over 500,000 square miles (1,300,000 sq km) of Mexican land, nearly all of the land that now makes up New Mexico, Utah, Nevada, Arizona, California, Texas, and western Colorado.

Brigham Young notified President Polk in 1846 that the Mormons were leaving the country.

> [W]hile we appreciate the Constitution of the United States as the most precious among the nations, we feel that we had rather retreat to the deserts, islands or mountain caves than consent to be ruled by governors and judges whose hands are drenched in the blood of innocence and virtue, who delight in injustice and oppression.

In the middle of winter, Young led 2,000 followers across the frozen Mississippi River and into brutal conditions in southern

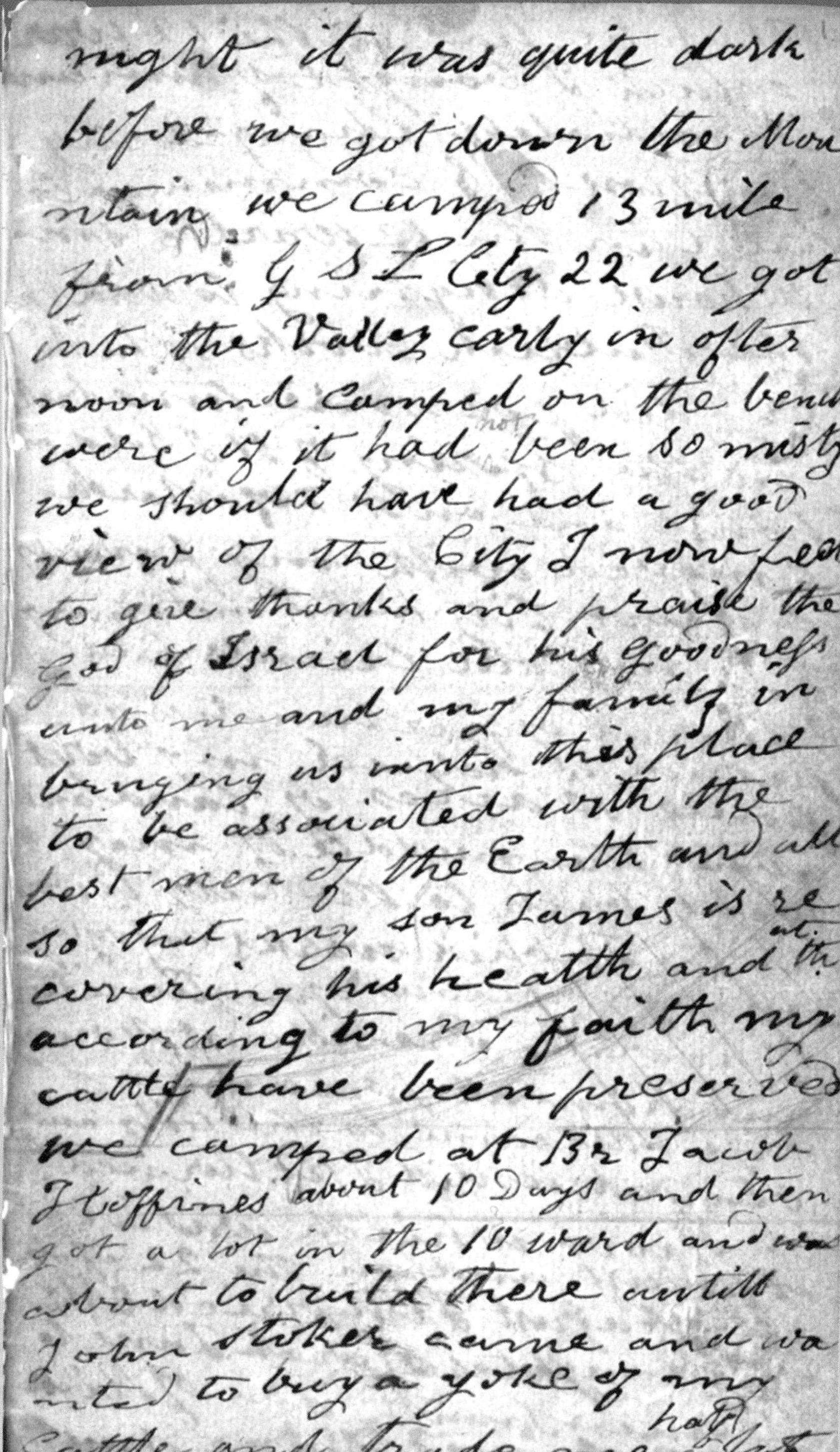

night it was quite dark
before we got down the Mou
ntain we camped 13 mile
from G S L City 22 we got
into the Valley early in after
noon and Camped on the bench
were if it had not been so misty
we should have had a good
view of the City I now feel
to give thanks and praise the
God of Israel for his goodness
unto me and my family in
bringing us into this place
to be associated with the
best men of the Earth and all
so that my son James is re
covering his health and that
according to my faith my
cattle have been preserved
we camped at Br Jacob
Hoffines about 10 Days and then
got a lot in the 10 ward and was
about to build there untill
John Stoker came and wa
nted to buy a yoke of my
cattle and trade me a half lot

English native Jonathan Oldham Duke (1807–1868) converted to the Mormon faith in 1839 and journeyed on the land trail to Salt Lake City, Utah. His handwritten diary and autobiography, from which a page is shown above, reveal in detail the religious persecution he faced and his difficult passage west to freedom. See transcription of this diary page on page 57.

Iowa. After reading Captain John Frémont's extensive reports of travel in the West, Young decided that the place for his people was the Great Salt Lake valley. At the time, the Utah Territory belonged to Mexico, and Young figured that the Mexican government would let them live in peace.

To avoid other caravans, the 73 Mormon wagons and 148 people stayed north of the Oregon Trail. The Mormon Trail crossed the Missouri River at Council Bluffs and followed the north side of the Platte, just across the river from the Oregon Trail. Along the way, the travelers placed signposts to mark the trail for later groups of Mormons. The Mormon Trail joined with the Oregon Trail along the snow-covered south banks of the Sweetwater River and up through South Pass, reaching Fort Bridger in southern Wyoming by early July. At Fort Bridger, the Mormons took a left turn toward California.

The trail became much worse, and the underfed people and their animals were extremely tired from the hard travel through the mountainous territory. A fever swept through the caravan, even catching Brigham Young. On July 19, Young stopped the caravan at the banks of the Weber River in the Utah Territory. He sent Orson Pratt and a small party to dig a trail through to the Great Salt Lake valley. On July 22, 1847, a member of Pratt's group wrote in his diary, "We have opened a road thru the kanyon where it is uncertain whether man or beast ever trod before unless it be a bear or a rattlesnake." Two days later, Young's wagon arrived. He lifted the back flap, regarded the beautiful meadow at the bottom of a canyon sliced by rushing creeks, and said, "This is the place."

The Mormons had forged a new trail off the Oregon Trail into Utah. By September 1847, another 400 Mormon families and

5,000 head of livestock had arrived in Salt Lake City, leading Young to write,

> We have fulfilled the mission ... by selecting and pointing out to you a beautiful site for a city, which is destined to be a place of refuge for the oppressed, and one that is calculated to please the eye, to cheer the heart, and fill the hungry soul with food.

In the following decade, over 60,000 Mormons moved west in hopes of building a Mormon nation. Yet, their dream of an independent nation did not last. Despite regular skirmishes between the Mormons and the U.S. Army, Utah became an American territory in 1850. Forty-six years after that, Utah was convinced to join the Union as its forty-fifth state.

The Donner Party

While the first Mormon party suffered many hardships on the trail, theirs were small in comparison to the gruesome fate of the Donner-Reed party. In May 1846, the Donner-Reed wagon train hit the Oregon Trail headed for California. It was late in the year to be starting. Ignoring the advice of experienced mountain men at Fort Bridger, the leaders of the train turned south to take a shortcut to California. They did not reach the base of the Sierra Nevada until late October.

In the shadow of 12,000-foot (3,658-m) peaks, the wagon train hauled through snowdrifts taller than a human. The train began to spread apart. By November, the snow was fifteen feet (4.6 m) deep. Near Lake Tahoe, the Donner group found an abandoned cabin and used fallen timber to build shelters. Cattle froze in their sleep. Frostbite and starvation began to claim lives. When the animals were too frozen to thaw and no food remained, the Donner party began to eat the flesh of their own dead.

By the time they were rescued in late February, approximately forty-three of the original eighty-seven people were dead. If they had left Missouri in March instead of May, theirs would have been a different history.

The best time to head out on the Oregon Trail from Missouri was as soon as the snow thawed in the spring. For some unfortunate caravans, such as the Donner Party, waiting until May had dangerous consequences:

- The grass on the trail would be eaten by the animals of earlier caravans. Later caravans had to wander far from the trail to feed their animals, which slowed them down.

- The Missouri River and other rivers often flooded in the spring and summer. Early starters could avoid the worst of it.

- Over the course of spring and summer, the trail was worn down by the wheel ruts and hooves of passing animals, slowing later caravans.

Slowdowns across the Great Plains forced caravans to cross the Rocky Mountains closer to winter, when colder temperatures and heavier snowfall could kill animals and strand caravans.

Gold, Gold, Gold!

On January 24, 1848, James S. Brown was working the whipsaw at Sutter's Mill in California when foreman James Marshall approached. Brown later wrote of the moment:

[H]ere came Mr. Marshall with his old wool hat in hand, and stopped within six or eight yards of the saw pit, and

"Methods of Mining" was one of a series of pictorial letter sheets published by James Hutchings in his 1855 *Hutchings' California Scenes*. The page's illustrations depict views of the major types of gold mining practiced in California at that time, including hydraulic washing, sluicing, panning, tunneling, cradling, and building flumes.

exclaimed, "Boys, I have got her now." I, being the nearest to him, and having more curiosity than the rest of the men, jumped from the pit and stepped to him, and on looking in his hat discovered say ten or twelve pieces of small scales of what proved to be gold.

From these nuggets, the California gold rush was born. Stories spread claiming that men were shoveling up gold by the sack. Before the rivers had thawed, men were scrambling for supplies in St. Joseph and Westport, eager to hit the Oregon Trail.

While thousands of Americans streamed out onto the Oregon Trail in the summer of 1848, the U.S. Senate approved the Treaty of Guadalupe Hidalgo, which ended the Mexican-American War and turned California into an American territory. The trail to California was now protected by the U.S. government. At the end of it lay, many believed, a large pot of gold.

Many of those poorly prepared gold diggers had neither time nor patience for fellow travelers on the trail. When unnecessary items had to be dropped to lighten the load, they were burned so that other gold rushers could not use them. Few of those gold diggers found any gold. By 1853, the gold rush was over. Those who came afterward were in search of business opportunities, good farmlands, or just a fresh start in the new state of California.

The State of Oregon

By 1850, Mexico had been pushed out of California and the Southwest. Great Britain had agreed to stay north of the forty-ninth parallel. Utah had been settled. In Oregon, the Donation Land Law of 1850 provided up to 640 acres (259 ha) of land to families willing to settle there.

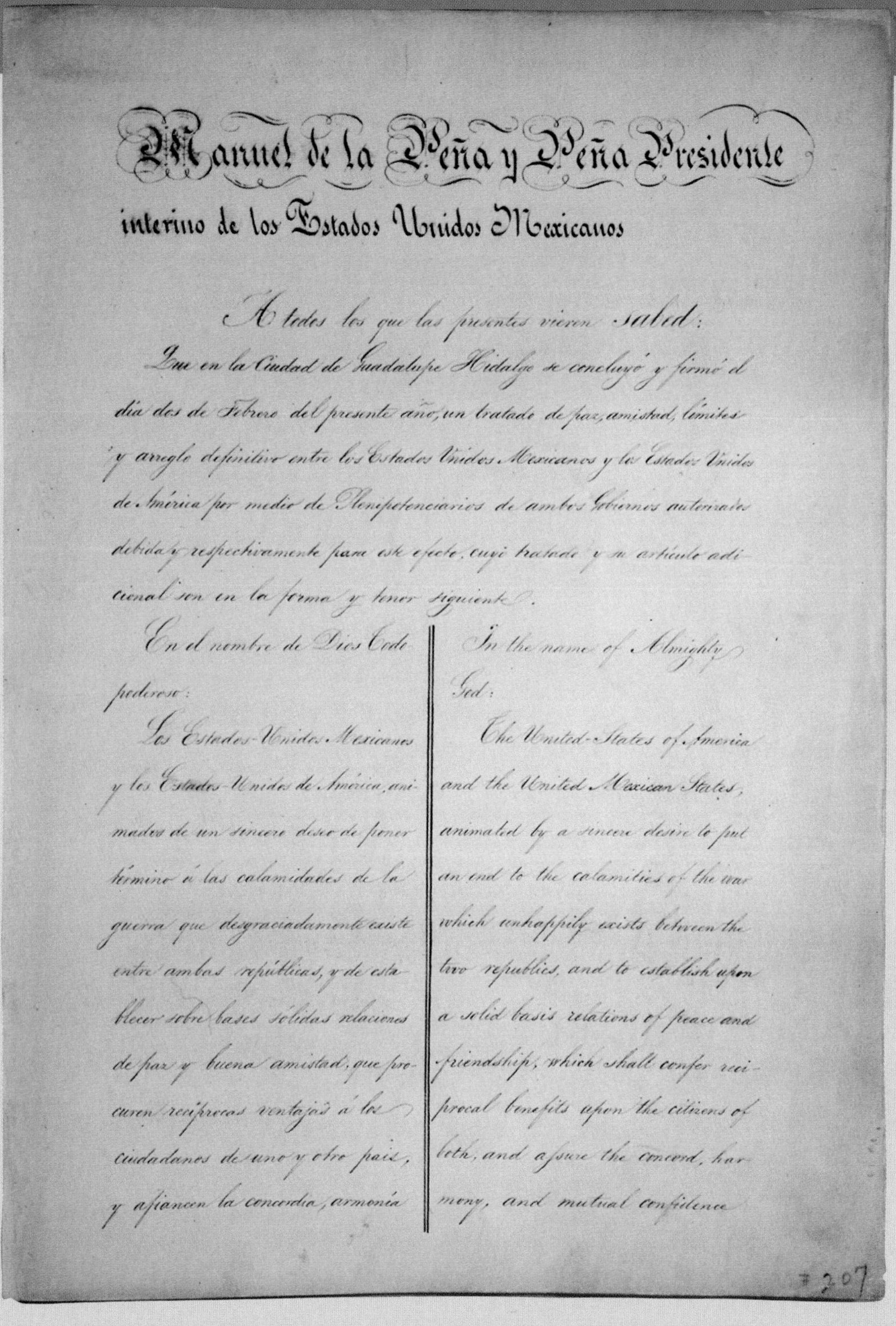
Manuel de la Peña y Peña Presidente
interino de los Estados Unidos Mexicanos

A todos los que las presentes vieren sabed:

Que en la Ciudad de Guadalupe Hidalgo se concluyó y firmó el dia dos de Febrero del presente año, un tratado de paz, amistad, límites y arreglo definitivo entre los Estados Unidos Mexicanos y los Estados Unidos de América por medio de Plenipotenciarios de ambos Gobiernos autorizados debida y respectivamente para este efecto, cuyo tratado y su artículo adicional son en la forma y tenor siguiente.

En el nombre de Dios Todo poderoso:

Los Estados-Unidos Mexicanos y los Estados-Unidos de América, animados de un sincero deseo de poner término á las calamidades de la guerra que desgraciadamente existe entre ambas repúblicas, y de establecer sobre bases sólidas relaciones de paz y buena amistad, que procuren recíprocas ventajas á los ciudadanos de uno y otro país, y afiancen la concordia, armonía

In the name of Almighty God:

The United-States of America and the United Mexican States, animated by a sincere desire to put an end to the calamities of the war which unhappily exists between the two republics, and to establish upon a solid basis relations of peace and friendship, which shall confer reciprocal benefits upon the citizens of both, and assure the concord, harmony, and mutual confidence

#207

The Treaty of Guadalupe Hidalgo, shown above, was signed on February 2, 1848, thus ending the Mexican-American War. The treaty also drew the U.S.-Mexican border and allowed the United States to purchase a large mass of land, which set the final shape of the country (that is, until the additions of Hawaii and Alaska). With the addition of new land came questions of slavery, and it wasn't long before the United States drove itself into a civil war. **See transcription excerpt on page 57.**

To Native Americans, these were all troubling signs. They knew the flood of settlers would not stop. In an effort to ensure peace, the First Laramie Treaty was signed in 1851 between the U.S. Army and nine of the thirteen Plains tribes. In exchange for protected tribal hunting grounds, white Americans were allowed safe passage along the Oregon Trail.

The peace did not last. The rising number of white settlers, their ignorance of sacred grounds, the spread of disease, and the massacre of buffalo angered many tribes. Raiding parties from formerly peaceful tribes stole horses, burned wagons, and sometimes killed settlers. The survivors demanded protection from the U.S. Army. Over a series of battles in the 1850s, the superior numbers and weapons of the U.S. Army began to weaken native tribes and pushed them out of the way of the thundering herd of white settlers.

By the end of the decade, the caravans on the Oregon Trail had begun to thin out, and in 1859, Oregon became a state.

CHAPTER 5

During the Civil War (1861–1865), the Oregon Trail was quiet as the young men who might have scouted ahead, hunted game and negotiated with traders were dying on battlefields like Bull Run and Gettysburg. Other events during the 1860s signaled the end of travel by wagon on the Oregon Trail.

THE END OF AN ERA

In January 27, 1860, businessman William Russell telegraphed his son, "Have determined to establish a pony express to Sacramento, California . . . Time ten days." His company, Russell, Majors, & Waddell, hoped that the Pony Express would speed delivery of the mail in the West.

On April 3, a young rider in a red shirt hopped onto the saddle of a horse and raced west from St. Joseph, Missouri, along the Oregon Trail toward Wyoming. The Pony Express was born. Day and night, each rider rode 30 to 50 miles (48 to 80 km) on three different horses with a two-minute break between rides. Ten days later, a rider thundered into Sacramento,

This poster advertises the services of the Pony Express, promising that messages could travel from New York to San Francisco in only nine days. The daring and adventurous riders employed by the Pony Express (there were nearly 100 in all) ranged in age from eleven to forty-four. They were required to weigh less than 125 pounds (57 kilograms), in order to lessen the burden on the horses, which were changed every 15 miles (24 km) or so. For their work, the riders earned $100 per month.

PONY EXPRESS.

Nine Days from San Francisco to New York

 THE CENTRAL Overland Pony Express Company will start their LETTER EXPRESS from San Francisco to New York and intermediate points,

On Tuesday, the 3d day of April ne t,

And upon every Tuesday thereafter, at 4 o'clock P. M.

Letters will be received at San Francisco until 3¾ o'clock each day of departure.

OFFICE—

Alta Telegraph Office, Montgomery st.,

Telegraphic Dispatches will be received at Carson City until 6 o'clock P. M., every Wednesday.

SCHEDULE TIME FROM SAN FRANCISCO TO NEW YORK.

For Telegraphic Dispatches...............................Nine Days
For Letters...Thirteen Days

Letters will be charged, between San Francisco and Salt Lake City, $3 per half ounce and under, and at that rate according to weight.

To all points beyond Salt Lake City, $5 per half ounce and under, and at that rate according to weight.

Telegraphic Dispatches will be subject to the same charges as letters.

All letters must be inclosed in stamped envelopes.

WM. W. FINNEY,

m18   Agent C. O P. E. Co.

By March preparations were so far advanced that advertisements began to appear in leading newspapers throughout the country. The Evening Bulletin of San Francisco printed this ad.

California, and another arrived on schedule back in St. Joseph. The feat thrilled America.

The Pony Express lasted only eighteen months. On October 24, 1861, the transcontinental telegraph was completed. Instead of sending mail overland by Pony Express, messages could be delivered to the West Coast in a matter of minutes and for less money. The firm of Russell, Majors, & Waddell had counted on mail delivery to support their business. The firm went bankrupt, and the coaches and horses were sold at auction.

Railroad Completed

In the East, railroads had already proven to be valuable to trade, travel, and mail delivery. Beginning in the 1840s, businessmen and government leaders argued over the construction costs, the benefits, and the building of a railroad across the country. In 1857, Theodore Judah, a civil engineer in San Francisco, presented a plan for building the railroad, including an argument for private funding of the project.

No one doubts that a liberal appropriation [use] of money or of public lands by the General Government, ought to insure the construction of this Railroad, but the proposition carries the elements of its destruction with it; it is the house divided against itself; it cannot be done until the route is defined; and, if defined, the opposing interest is powerful enough to defeat it.

Judah's plan eventually arrived on the desk of Leland Stanford, who hired Judah to select a route over the Sierra Nevada. Stanford formed a company with Sacramento businessmen Collis P. Huntington, Mark Hopkins, and Charles Crocker.

The completion of the Union Pacific Railroad, the first transcontinental railroad, made the Oregon Trail unnecessary as a means of travel across the United States. This photograph shows steam locomotives on Devil's Gate Bridge during construction of the Union Pacific. A construction miracle, the railroad joined California with the East, bringing together what seemed like two separate nations.

In 1862, the Union Pacific Railway project led by these four businessmen was chartered. With the railroad project underway, the government passed the Homestead Act to encourage settlers to claim farmlands in the West. By claiming farmlands near the proposed route of the railroad, farmers could load their crops and animals onto the railroad to send to markets in the East.

On May 10, 1869, at Promontory, Utah, Leland Stanford drove a gold spike through a Union Pacific and a Central Pacific rail to complete the transcontinental railroad. The West and the East were joined.

Other achievements and inventions sped the development of the West. In 1868, James Oliver developed a steel plow that was sharp enough to cut through the hard soil of the Plains states. Farming communities began to flourish along the railroad routes. The invention of barbed wire allowed farmers to protect their crops from wild animals and cattle herds. Other railroads in the West, such as the Oregon Shortline, joined with the Union Pacific to knit the nation together.

By 1900, the Oregon Trail was gone. Brush had crawled back onto the paths. The wheel ruts had filled with grass and weeds. For settlers coming west, the days in the hot sun, under the threat of sandstorms, disease, animal bites, and attacks by Native Americans had been replaced by a few days' ride in the comforts of a passenger train. And in a few decades, the train would be replaced as well. Those who came west drove the interstate.

The Next Trail

It is estimated that nearly 500,000 people came west over the Oregon Trail. Thousands died trying to do so. Over the span of a single lifetime, the first white Americans reached the Pacific by land, and the entire West Coast joined the United States. In a single lifetime, paths made by animal tracks along this route had become railroad tracks, and cities like Kansas City, Laramie, and Portland began to bloom along the Oregon Trail.

What trails will be pioneered in this lifetime? While every mountain and every river in the United States has been mapped, American pioneers will find new routes into the unknown and pave them for the rest to follow.

PRIMARY SOURCE TRANSCRIPTIONS

Page 8: Louisiana Purchase Treaty

Transcription/Translation of Excerpt
Article I

Whereas by the Article the third of the Treaty concluded at St Ildefonso the 9th Vendé miaire an 9/1st October 1800 between the First Consul of the French Republic and his Catholic Majesty it was agreed as follows.

"His Catholic Majesty promises and engages on his part to cede to the French Republic six months after the full and entire execution of the conditions and Stipulations herein relative to his Royal Highness the Duke of Parma, the Colony or Province of Louisiana with the Same extent that it now has in the hand of Spain, & that it had when France possessed it; and Such as it Should be after the Treaties subsequently entered into between Spain and other States."

And whereas in pursuance of the Treaty and particularly of the third article the French Republic has an incontestible title to the domain and to the possession of the said Territory–The First Consul of the French Republic desiring to give to the United States a strong proof of his friendship doth hereby cede to the United States in the name of the French Republic for ever and in full Sovereignty the said territory with all its rights and appurtenances as fully and in the Same manner as they have been acquired by the French Republic in virtue of the above mentioned Treaty concluded with his Catholic Majesty.

Page 30: Letter of Instructions from Thomas Jefferson to Meriwether Lewis

Transcription of Excerpt
June 20 1803

The commerce which may be carried on with the people inhabiting the line you will pursue, renders a knolege of those people important. You will therefore endeavour to make yourself acquainted, as far as a diligent pursuit of your journey shall admit, with the names of the nations & their numbers; the extent & limits of their possessions; their relations with other tribes of nations; their language, traditions, monuments; their ordinary occupations in agriculture, fishing, hunting, war, arts & the implements for these; their food, clothing, & domestic accomodations; the diseases prevalent among them, & the remedies they use; moral & physical circumstances which distinguish them from the tribes we know; peculiarities in their laws, customs & dispositions; and articles of commerce they may need or furnish & to what extent.

And considering the interest which every nation has in extending & strengthening the authority of reason & justice among the people around them, it will be useful to acquire what knolege you can of the state of morality, religion, & information among them; as it may better enable those who may endeavor to civilize & instruct them, to adapt their measures to the existing notions & practices of those on whom they are to operate.

In all your intercourse with the natives, treat them in the most friendly & conciliatory manner which their own conduct will admit; allay all jealousies as to the object of your journey, satisfy them of its innocence, make them acquainted with the position, extent character, peaceable & commercial dispositions of the US. of our wish to be neighborly, friendly, & useful to them, & of our dispositions to a commercial intercourse with them; confer with them on the points most convenient as mutual emporiums, and the articles of most desireable interchange for them & us. If a few of their influential chiefs within practicable distance, wish to visit us, arrange such a visit with them, and furnish them with authority to call on our officers, on their entering the US. to have them conveyed to this place at the public expence. If any of them should wish to have some of their young people brought up with us, & taught such arts as may be useful to them, we will recieve, instruct & take care of them. Such a mission whether of influential chiefs or of young people would give some security to your own party. Carry with you some matter of the kinepox; inform those of them with whom you may be, of it's efficacy as a preservative from the smallpox; & instruct & encourage them in the use of it. This may be especially done wherever you winter.

As it is impossible for us to foresee in what manner you will be recieved by those people, whether with hospitality or hostility, so is it impossible to prescribe the exact degree of preserverance with which you are to pursue your journey. We value too much the lives of citizens to offer them to probable destruction. Your numbers will be sufficient to secure you against the unauthorised opposition of individuals or of small parties: but if a superior force authorised, or not authorised by a nation, should be arrayed against your further passage, and inflexibly determined to arrest it, you must decline it's farther pursuit, and return. In the loss of yourselves, we should lose also the information you will have acquired. By returning safely with that, you may enable us to renew the essay with better calculated means. To your own discretion therefore must be left the degree of danger you risk, and the point at which you should decline, only saying we wish you to err on the side of your safety, and to bring back your party safe even if it be with less information.

Page 42: Jonathan Oldham Duke Diary Page

Transcription of Diary Page

night it was quite dark before we got down the Mountain we camped 13 mile from G S L City 22 we got into the Valley early in after noon and camped on the bench were if it had been so misty we should have had a good view of the City I now feel to give thanks and praise the God of Israel for his goodness unto me and my family in bringing us innto this place to be associated with the best men of the Earth and all so that my son James is recovering his health and that according to my faith my cattle have been preserved we camped at Br Jacob Hoffines about 10 Days and then got a lot in the 10 ward and w{illegible->} [- - -] about to build there untill John Stoker came and wanted to buy a yoke of my cattle and trade me a half lot . . .

Page 48: Treaty of Guadalupe Hidalgo

Transcription of Excerpt

IN THE NAME OF ALMIGHTY GOD The United States of America and the United Mexican States animated by a sincere desire to put an end to the calamities of the war which unhappily exists between the two Republics and to establish Upon a solid basis relations of peace and friendship, which shall confer reciprocal benefits upon the citizens of both, and assure the concord, harmony, and mutual confidence wherein the two people should live. . .

GLOSSARY

botany The study of plant life.

caravan A group of wagons and horses that travel together for safety.

cholera A disease transmitted through contaminated food or water.

Continental Divide A ridge of high land that runs from Alaska to Mexico. Rivers on the east side of the line flow to the east, while rivers on the west side flow toward the Pacific Ocean.

emigrant A person who moves out of a country or region.

frontiersman A man who has experience and skills in living in frontier areas.

Great Plains An enormous expanse of flat grasslands that stretches across the states of the Midwest.

Hidatsa The language spoken by the Mandan tribe.

keelboat A flat-bottomed boat suitable for navigating rivers.

nomadic Roaming from place to place.

pioneer Someone who is among the first to accomplish a challenging feat.

prairie schooner A nickname for the wagons used by emigrants to cross the Oregon Trail.

reservation Plots of poor-quality land where Native American tribes were herded as white Americans took over their land.

South Pass Discovered by Robert Stuart, the South Pass through the Wind River Range in Wyoming permitted easy passage for wagons and horses across the Continental Divide.

tariff A fee.

transcontinental Something that crosses a continent.

trapper A mountain man who caught beavers and otters in traps to sell their pelts.

vermillion Bright red pigment.

zoology The study of animal life.

FOR MORE INFORMATION

Bureau of Indian Affairs
1849 C Street NW, Suite 4160
Washington, DC 20240
(202) 208-7581
Web site: http://www.doiu.nbc.gov/orientation/bia2.cfm

Lewis and Clark Trail Heritage Foundation
P.O. Box 3434
Great Falls, MT 59403
(888) 701-3434
Web site: http://www.lewisandclark.org

Missouri Historical Society
P.O. Box 11940
St. Louis, MO 63112-0040
Web site: http://www.mohistory.org

Oregon Historical Society
1200 SW Park Avenue
Portland, OR 97203
(503) 222-1741
Web site: http://www.ohs.org

Web Sites

Due to the changing nature of Internet links, the Rosen Publishing
Group, Inc., has developed an online list of Web sites related to the
subject of this book. This site is updated regularly. Please use this link
to access the list:

http://www.rosenlinks.com/psah/ortr

FOR FURTHER READING

Fisher, Leonard Everett. *The Oregon Trail*. New York: Holiday
House, 1990.

Place, Marian T. *Westward on the Oregon Trail*. New York: American
Heritage Publishing Co., Inc., 1962.

Stein, R. Conrad. *Lewis and Clark*. New York: Grolier Children's
Press, 1994.

BIBLIOGRAPHY

Applegate, Jesse. *A Day with the Cow Column*. Chicago: Printed for the Caxton Club, 1934.

Coffman, Lloyd W. *Blazing a Wagon Trail to Oregon: A Weekly Chronicle of the Great Migration of 1843*. Springfield, OR: Echo Books, 1993.

DeVoto, Bernard, ed. *The Journals of Lewis and Clark*. Boston: Houghton Mifflin Co., 1997.

Fisher, Leonard Everett. *The Oregon Trail*. New York: Holiday House, 1990.

Place, Marian T. *Westward on the Oregon Trail*. New York: American Heritage Publishing Co., Inc., 1962.

Roberts, B. H. *Comprehensive History of the Church of Jesus Christ of the Latter Day Saints*. Salt Lake City: Brigham Young University Press, 1965.

Spaulding, Kenneth A. *On the Oregon Trail: Robert Stuart's Journey of Discovery*. Norman, OK: University of Oklahoma Press, 1953.

Stein, R. Conrad. *Lewis and Clark*. New York: Grolier Children's Press, 1994.

Talbot, Margaret. "Searching for Sacagawea." *National Geographic Magazine*, Vol. 203, No. 2, February 2003, pp. 68–85.

PRIMARY SOURCE IMAGE LIST

NDEX

About the Author

Steven P. Olson is a freelance writer whose ancestors came to California by wagon. His Web site is http://www.stevenolson.com.

Special Thanks

Map of the Oregon Trail provided by Annette Olson of Fineline Maps (http:// www.finelinemaps.com)

Photo Credits

Back cover (top left) © Bettmann/Corbis; back cover (top right, middle right), front cover, pp. 18, 27, 29, 41, 53 © Hulton/Archive/Getty Images; back cover (middle left) Pilgrim Hall Museum; back cover (bottom left), p. 51 © The Bridgeman Art Library; back cover (bottom right) William T. Clements Library, University of Michigan; p. 1 © Geoffrey Clements/Corbis; pp. 6-7 © Annette Olson; pp. 8, 48 National Archives and Records Administration; p. 14 Smithsonian Institution, National Museum of American History, Behting Center, Washington, DC; pp. 16, 30 Thomas Jefferson Papers, Manuscript Division, Library of Congress; p. 20 Rare Book and Special Collections Division, Library of Congress; p. 22 © American Philosophical Society; p. 25 © Christie's Images/The Bridgeman Art Library; p. 28 The Denver Public Library, Western History Collection; p. 33 © James L. Amos/Corbis; pp. 36, 42 Harold B. Lee Library, Brigham Young University; p. 38 © Corbis; p. 46 The Bancroft Library, University of California, Berkeley.

Designer: Nelson Sá; Editor: Christine Poolos; Photo Researcher: Adriana Skura